Your Complete Forecast 2018 Horoscope

LIBRA

Your Complete Forecast 2018 Horoscope

LIBRA

BEJAN DARUWALLA
With
NASTUR DARUWALLA

Ranvir Books
HARPER element

First published in India in 2017 by Harper Element
An imprint of HarperCollins *Publishers*

P-ISBN: 978-93-5277-342-8
E-ISBN: 978-93-5277-343-5

2 4 6 8 10 9 7 5 3 1

HarperCollins *Publishers*
A-75, Sector 57, Noida, Uttar Pradesh 201301, India
1 London Bridge Street, London, SE1 9GF, United Kingdom
2 Bloor Street East, Toronto, Ontario M4W 1A8, Canada
Lvl 13, 201 Elizabeth Street (PO Box A565, NSW, 1235), Sydney
NSW 2000, Australia
195 Broadway, New York, NY 10007, USA

Typeset in 11.5/15 Sabon
By Saanvi Graphics, Noida

Printed and bound at
MicroPrints (India), New Delhi

Contents

LIBRA

23 September–22 October

Life can be a necklace of glittering rubies and diamonds, each gem in its own brilliance, and dancing in radiance with all the others.

- **Element:** Air
- **Ruling planet:** Venus
- **Colours:** Blue, jade green
- **Metal:** Copper
- **Scents:** Almond, rose, vanilla, violet
- **Quality:** Cardinal (=activity)
- **Deepest needs:** Love, romance, social harmony
- **Characteristics to avoid:** Violating what is right in order to be socially accepted
- **Day:** Friday

SPECIAL MESSAGE FROM BEJAN AND NASTUR

In ancient times Virgo, Libra and Scorpio were one sign. My special observation is that all these three signs are very choosy and fussy about food, health and may have phobias. I repeat that they *may* have phobias. I do not say that all of them have definite phobias. Librans have an inherent need to act democratically, diplomatically and fairly. Adversely afflicted, they have trouble in making decisions and may lose themselves in sensual pleasures. In highly evolved Librans, the human mind finds the perfect blend between balance and discretions.

JUPITER

Jupiter will be in your second angle from 10 October 2017 to 8 November

2018. Jupiter is the heavyweight of the zodiac. Jupiter has everything to do with finance, family, food, taste, clothes, knowledge, education, servants, wealth, physical enjoyments, buying and selling, earning through your own efforts and acquisitions from father. Jupiter actually gives you a silver tongue as the Americans say. So, dear suave and diplomatic Librans, you know what to expect from Jupiter in 2018. Wow!

SATURN

By Western astrology, Saturn will be in your fourth angle from 21 December 2017 to 22 March 2020. Saturn is a spoilsport, a killjoy, a wet blanket. In other words, Saturn spoils the fun and the joy of life. Therefore, you will not get all the happy results of the fourth house. For elderly people, Saturn in the fourth angle will mark the end of a relationship which has been going on for a long time. The emphasis will very definitely be on local, family and domestic frontiers. Saturn is a lame old man. Therefore, Saturn represents old people like parents and elders. Saturn is also a teacher. Therefore, Saturn also represents gurus and mentors. Saturn, by both Indian and Western astrology, stands for duties and responsibilities. So, it is very clear that your responsibilities and duties will increase many times over. Be prepared to shoulder them. You Librans have balance and poise. It will help you in every possible way.

If you are young at heart you can start making a blueprint of your profession and accomplishments. It will be the right time to amend and stitch up all pending issues and matters. Also, if you have made commitments, it is time to fulfil them.

Saturn by nature is objective and rational and does not like to be too personal and subjective. I would naturally advice you not be very personal and as far as possible be objective, rational, clear-headed. The other features are house, home, property, renovation and decoration, alteration, mining, gardening, farming. The list is endless. I will make it very simple. Anything to do with land and property will come into sharp focus. I am sure you do understand this very well.

For you Librans, Venus, the planet of beauty, money, honey, is the main planet. Venus will help you in creativity hobbies from 18 January to 12 February and from 7 to 30 March. Relationships will matter the most. From 25 April to 19 May journeys, travel, ceremonies, foreign affairs, matters related to parents will claim your attention. From 14 June to 9 July you will combine business and pleasure, entertainment and profit. This is a really a fine period for you. From 7 August to 8 September you will try to analyse and introspect your own self, and at the same time fan out to other people. In other words, you will be doing many things at the same time. The best part of it is that this last prediction will be repeated between 1 November to 2 December for you.

In 2018, Saturn and Jupiter will be in an excellent formation. Therefore, I suggest that you should try to get the best out of the year. You should ring it dry.

URANUS

On and after 4 March 2019 Uranus moves out of your seventh angle. This is a blessing. The reason is Uranus screws up your relationships in one way or another. Uranus disrupts and changes everything. In other words, the year 2018 will be the last one of changes. These changes could mean separations, lawsuits, legal affairs, opposition to parents and so on. Fortunately, you

Librans are charming and polished, and therefore you will be hurt less than those of other signs by Uranus.

NEPTUNE

Neptune will be in your eighth angle till 2024. But in 2018, very specially, Neptune will turn on your intuition, imagination, psychic powers, dreams and so on. Also, Neptune will augment your income by different sources and that is certainly very important. These sources could be rent, factory, industry, job, profession, business, freelancing. To put it simply you will get money in different ways.

PLUTO

Pluto walks beside Saturn in your fourth angle and Pluto helps Saturn to walk a little faster and give quicker results. Please read Saturn in your fourth angle once again. Everything said there will work at a quicker pace and be more beneficial at least by 50 per cent or so. Your former professor of English, now eighty-six years old, cannot resist the temptation of giving marks.

MONTHLY ROUND-UP

January: House, home, family;

February: Romance, children, creativity;
March: Work and health improvement measures;

April: Marriage, relationships, contacts, trips, ties and opposition;

May: Loans, funds, health, taxes, accidents, legal matters;

June: Publicity, publishing, fame, religious rites, matters to do with parents and in-laws;

July: Parents, in-laws, work, rewards, family, the effort you do put in;

August: Contacts and group activities, gains and joy;

September: Expenses, health, but also God's grace and success in ventures and fine connections, collaborations;

October: Confidence, success, charm;

November: Finances, family, food, fortune, the four Fs,

December: Communication and contacts at all levels.

HAPPINESS QUOTA: 76 per cent

WEEKLY REVIEW (BY PHASES OF THE MOON)

2 JANUARY: FULL MOON IN CANCER

You will be striving to achieve right from the word 'go'. You want to have the position and clout to go your own way, do what you like best. All this needs the power (either in terms of social/family status or money) and that's what you set out to get. For this, hard work is the only answer and that's what you're doing, in the new millennium, but with a set purpose in mind.

8 JANUARY: LAST QUARTER IN LIBRA

The word I spoke of, just above, centres on creative pursuits – always a focal point for Librans, in some form or other – as a means of earning. Hobbies too will be equally important. Your main concern will be your family, particularly your children, though parents and in-laws too play an important role. Moneymaking, in terms of speculation, playing the stock market, will be favoured, but don't be foolhardy.

17 JANUARY: NEW MOON IN CAPRICORN

Once again family matters, the health of older relatives, parents and in-laws is focused. Also, equally important will be matters pertaining to your house and property as a family holding. Hassles or problems not of your making but still yours to sort out will take time, effort, hard work, and needless to say, money as well. You've got your hands full this quarter. Your own health too will need safeguarding.

24 JANUARY: FIRST QUARTER IN TAURUS

There's a tremendous lightening up of the environment you're living in, a breath of spring in the heart of winter. I'm talking now about love and romance, joy, gaiety, laughter. You interact with people now, no longer ploughing a lonely furrow. Good times, the social whirligig, bring a measure of happiness, and ease the burdens you were weighed down by.

31 JANUARY: FULL MOON IN LEO

You will now shift your orientation from the social and family scene. It's money that will concern and occupy you, in terms of funds and investments, lending and borrowing for your own projects and enterprises. Your interactions with people will have to be at their best. Don't vitiate the atmosphere with confrontations, showdowns that can be avoided with tact. It's not the time to feel threatened by others. You need people for your own advancement, says Ganesha.

7 FEBRUARY: LAST QUARTER IN SCORPIO

Once again, money matters this week too. You'll have to attend to buying and selling, possessions and valuables, property and liquid assets. Don't be bulldozed into doing something you don't want to or let others trespass in your path. Family matters will demand that you be gentle but firm and stick up for yourself. Tact and charm will come in more handy for personal affairs that clamour for your attention. Ganesha warns you – a busy week.

15 FEBRUARY: NEW MOON IN AQUARIUS

It's a time to love and be loved, to have that touch of romance and moonlight in your life. And that's something that Librans can really excel at. It's part of their charming, caressing ways – both sexes, not just Libran women. Fun, recreation and joy with children, pleasure and the leisure to chase it. Sounds like dream time? But there's the harsh reality of money matters to be dealt with, investments to be made.

23 FEBRUARY: FIRST QUARTER IN GEMINI

Trade and travel will keep you more than busy. Yet you find the time since you already have the inclination towards higher concerns like world laws, an order in the universe, justice for mankind. Spirituality, New Age concepts and values could easily be your forte now.

2 MARCH: FULL MOON IN VIRGO

It'll be a time of worries for you. Home affairs and ever-rising demands on your purse keep your nose to the grindstone. Your mind and heart, though, soar to new heights of God realization, realization of the oneness of God and Self, and searching within for both. A life of meditation, quietude, contemplation will be doubly attractive. This trend will prevail for some weeks to come.

9 MARCH: LAST QUARTER IN SAGITTARIUS

Your contemplative tendencies will take a back seat for the moment. There will be worries in juxtaposition with wish-fulfilment and dreams realized. Love and hate come to you in equal measure too. In addition, there will be a fairly large amount of social interaction and also much activity at the workplace. All in all, to call it a busy week would be an understatement.

17 MARCH: NEW MOON IN PISCES

Your work, your own creative talents and productivity will figure largely now. Also, and this will be an 'ongoing exercise' in modern office jargon, larger issues and social causes. In the money angle, there is an easing of tension as loans and funds come through. But you need to exercise care and control over your food habits and health. Keep a watch over your temper and your tongue, though.

24 MARCH: FIRST QUARTER IN CANCER

All your hard work, I might even say your Herculean efforts of the past, will start paying off now, especially in the workplace. In relationships, there can be harsh words, frayed tempers to watch for, to prevent relationships from turning bitter. The health of an older relative or parents can cause you many anxious moments too. Moneywise, it's a time when you're reasonably flush with funds, so it eases the stress. Social standing, perks and benefits get a boost too.

31 MARCH: FULL MOON IN LIBRA

It's a time when nothing can stop your personal progress. I'm saying this at the outset with a purpose. You can just decide not to be too domineering and assertive, creating animosity where none exists. It's not a good time in the sense that betrayals, back-stabbing, or let-downs could happen anyway. What you need now is emotional balance.

8 APRIL: LAST QUARTER IN CAPRICORN

You will have to deal, once again, with family matters, the house and home, property. Renovation, decoration, construction, extension may be necessary. You change from within and this is reflected in the change for the better in relations with family and relatives, and in domestic issues. Both could hitherto have been more than bothersome.

16 APRIL: NEW MOON IN ARIES

Finance and romance, now. In matters financial it will be trade, buying and selling, and also partnerships, tie-ups, collaborations that are important. Legal issues, enforcement of the law, will also be important. Short journeys are likely. I'm sure I don't have to spell out the details vis-à-vis romance. You can do it yourself!

22 APRIL: FIRST QUARTER IN LEO

There will, once again, be both happy times and hard work. Your Libran tendency will be to have both in equal measure but it can be a 60:40 ratio, with the balance tilting either way, depending on your personal horoscope. The bad news is that there could be concern about an older person in the family – health-wise.

30 APRIL: FULL MOON IN SCORPIO

A fresh new look comes into your life – the glitter of money. There are several different ways in which you could find yourself pursuing the making of money – buying and selling, also contracts, negotiations, even commission agencies. You could be signing legal documents, instruments of understanding, handling loans. Also, there will be the glamour of a new, fashionable wardrobe and a healthy amount of entertaining.

8 MAY: LAST QUARTER IN AQUARIUS

There is a shift towards better times now. Better health, better prospects, also the mindset which lets you enjoy parties, social gatherings, interaction with children. Appreciate the arts, enjoy theatre, music, exhibitions, as well as your own individual interests and hobbies. The placing I spoke of at the outset may influence your attitude to others – resentment of others, or lack of consideration and care for loved ones.

15 MAY: NEW MOON IN TAURUS

Love and money, usually considered the two motivating factors the world over, are yours too. Money matters will revolve around loans, joint finance, shopping, investments. Basically, more opportunities to make money – perhaps a job switch. You surely don't need to have the details of the love angle spelt out, but even so the tilt is more towards passion, sex, rather than love.

22 MAY: FIRST QUARTER IN VIRGO

Your improved financial resources now permit you to indulge yourself, doing the things that please you. Hobbies, quality time and interaction with both children and friends, and above all, love. Perhaps an affair, a liaison or a lifetime bond. This will of course depend on the individual natal horoscope.

29 MAY: FULL MOON IN SAGITTARIUS

Other things were going for you in a wonderful way last month. Now, it's relationships and communication; interaction with friends, neighbours, relatives or the whole wide world; the signing of contracts; or just correspondence and contacts; and of course, the entire range of media available in the world of information technology.

6 JUNE: LAST QUARTER IN PISCES

It's time for action for you now, Libran, and sheer grinding hard work. The sphere will be the electronic media, information technology, website of your own. The time is favourable for you to successfully launch a new venture/project/enterprise based on new technology. If nothing else, perhaps just streamlining and updating your work system, office procedures, what have you, for greater efficiency and better communication.

13 JUNE: NEW MOON IN GEMINI

The action continues this week too. New fields of study, new avenues of research, inventions, innovations. The key word, you may have noticed, is *new*. Travel is a foregone conclusion. Also, a means of broadening your mind to new vistas of knowledge. You may have to attend interviews, conferences or a meeting, perhaps even chair a committee. The world at large beckons and draws you nearer.

20 JUNE: FIRST QUARTER IN VIRGO

Your mood undergoes a sea change – a whole new perspective is what you have. Contemplation and isolation draw you more. Seas, water sources like rivers and lakes will attract you. You will feel both tired, world-weary and restless. This could have been building up over the past few weeks. On a practical level, there could be trade and connections overseas, foreign collaborations that may be fruitful.

28 JUNE: FULL MOON IN CAPRICORN

Having thought things through in the quiet you were craving. You realize that for you home is where the heart is, in a slightly different twist to this saying. Family, bonding with loved ones, close relatives, the joys of home comforts, domestic bliss and ties are what you seek. Ties could also be with someone older and wiser.

6 JULY: LAST QUARTER IN ARIES

The give-and-take trend of the last quarter could be a monthly trend. Other ties like legal accords, collaborations and partnerships may now develop. These could cover both home and work. There is much satisfaction for you, even a degree of pleasure in both work and family matters. Ganesha has blessed you in an unobtrusive, pleasing, but very lasting manner.

13 JULY: NEW MOON IN CANCER

You finally got the hang of it – I mean, what constitutes true success. You realize, like I did long ago, I must confess, that it comes from getting the most out of life. Not necessarily in money or material terms. You will give the best of yourself to both family and profession. And in doing so, make the best use of your time, energy, resources. There is a freshness in your methods that brings joy to the most mundane of tasks.

19 JULY: FIRST QUARTER IN LIBRA

You are in the frame of mind now that makes you want to assess, evaluate, even calculate your own achievements. These could be external or inner growth. A new, responsible *you* emerges, even diplomatic but more outgoing, more caring. Perhaps these are new heights of excellence or achievement, after all. Assignment, commitments, projects are successfully dealt with now.

27 JULY: FULL MOON IN AQUARIUS

The theme will definitely be ties. The growth you have experienced within you over the last weeks sets your feet firmly on the road to new bonds and ties – of love, of duty, of family, or of legal ties at work. You will need to be flexible, adaptable, open, in order to make them work – both at home and at the workplace. You'll do brilliantly at creative pursuits like the arts, music and theatre, a touch of drama, in speculation and investment, hobbies and even cinema and the media.

4 AUGUST: LAST QUARTER IN TAURUS

There is a danger of pursuing wrong career objective, even being irresponsible in your approach to work. The reason could be some anxiety, neurosis, niggling ailments, feeling out of sorts, which could tempt you to make the wrong moves now. The highlights will be passion and sex, loans and funds, and paradoxically, religion and spirituality.

11 AUGUST: NEW MOON IN LEO

It's the right time, perhaps even the best time for family and social activities, even perhaps so much of the latter that you could neglect dear ones and well-wishers. Old and new friends will be important. You are outgoing, friendly, classy, amiable. It's the ideal time to ask for favours. The success rate will be high, but you'll have to respond similarly when it's necessary to help others. Nothing comes for free.

18 AUGUST: FIRST QUARTER IN SCORPIO

You'll be doing two things that will make life smoother right now, and also augur well for the future. On the one hand, entertaining, friends, social gatherings; and on the other, a revamp or overhaul of finances and career/profession. There will be risks of spending too much on business concerns, in an attempt to raise your income.

26 AUGUST: FULL MOON IN PISCES

Ganesha now impels you to a bout of introspection. You could also be strongly into healing, succouring, nursing those who need it. In the process, of course, you will yourself be healed and helped out of the angst, neuroses that could overcome you. Self-analysis will draw you more than material concerns; also charitable work, welfare concerns. It's you as part of the larger community that is stressed now by Ganesha.

3 SEPTEMBER: LAST QUARTER IN GEMINI

Philosophical pursuits, questions of law and order, social justice, research, the environment will keep you drawn towards them. Travel will be a release and a learning experience too. There will be visits, meetings, interviews, conferences and publicity too. Interfacing with people is the keynote, be it collaborations or networking in a larger framework, or even just in-laws and both near and distant relatives.

9 SEPTEMBER: NEW MOON IN VIRGO

The introspective life, the passions of the mind once again. The monthly trend continues. Insights into life, cosmic questions, karmic laws, psychology. Once again, welfare, charity, healing and helping will keep you very busy. There may be a tendency in all this to dream up troubles, or try and carry the world's problems on your shoulders.

16 SEPTEMBER: FIRST QUARTER IN SAGITTARIUS

You will now be in the mood to break new horizons, get a new slant on life. The unique, the different, always hold an attraction for Librans in their quest for harmony. Travel and information technology will be interesting for you, especially the Net. Don't be too proud to ask for help, when needed. Also important are trips and ties with neighbours, relatives, friends.

25 SEPTEMBER: FULL MOON IN ARIES

Your mind is fixed on gentler paths, and your mood more mellow, romantic and affectionate. Travel for pleasure or work, renewal of old partnerships or forming fresh ones, romantic ties and attachments too, perhaps leading up to marriage, will be in the focus. So, trips and ties could sum it up best, and it's a trend for the coming birth month as well.

2 OCTOBER: LAST QUARTER IN CANCER

You will suddenly be like a nuclear powerhouse in terms of both energy levels and activity. The astrological reason, besides it being your birth month, is the long-range effect of the planets. You will be dynamic, setting a punishing pace, meeting targets, deadlines, achieving seemingly impossible height of energy and power!

9 OCTOBER: NEW MOON IN LIBRA

In your birth month, with the charge of energy you seem to have miraculously received, you will not only look at the brighter side of things but also have much to be cheerful and excited about. The worst of your troubles will be over. Your attitude will attract success and achievement. You brighten up your life, more practically, with a mint-fresh new look, image, clothes. Positive thinking indeed, chuckles Ganesha.

16 OCTOBER: FIRST QUARTER IN CAPRICORN

House and home and domesticity have never seemed more pleasant to you. You love them, warts and all (I mean squabbles, hang-ups as well as fun times and joys). All the same, you'll be working more than hard, sights firmly fixed on where you plan to get. The energy for it has already come to you. Your stars say that you will really make things happen!

24 OCTOBER: FULL MOON IN TAURUS

All this and heaven too could well be the theme for the coming period. Flights of fancy, the supernatural, the esoteric, the metaphysical, life after death, the deeper meaning of life all possess your mind and intellect, now that the worries of day-to-day life are behind you. On this topic, let me just say that in addition to any or all of the above, financial matters will have to be dealt with – loans, funds, buying and selling, capital, joint finances, investments – any or all, once again.

31 OCTOBER: LAST QUARTER IN LEO

Once again, a total shift. It's not that you are weak-minded, vacillating between different ideas, but it's just that your sheer mental energy has to let off steam; in addition to it there's your thirst for knowledge and wisdom. It's excitement of a totally different kind now – relaxation, fun and games, recreation, partying and dancing the night away. There will be greater closeness and intimacy too with the special person(s) in your life, in your serious look at the lighter side of life!

7 NOVEMBER: NEW MOON IN SCORPIO

Financial matters will need both considering and attention. Taxes, additional income, revenues and rentals, family funds. Also, improving or acquiring property and assets. On the personal level, relationships will be supportive with much mutual give and take. Your outlook and environment both change and others will be cooperative and sharing, bowled over by your charm!

15 NOVEMBER: FIRST QUARTER IN AQUARIUS

Getting things will be important. Also, relationships full of reciprocity, love, warmth. You will be cherished, treasured, especially in terms of bonding with children. Approaching nuptials too, yours or of someone very close to you. Yet again, plenty of physical activity, fitness regimes, sports and exercise so that you're on your toes both literally and figuratively.

23 NOVEMBER: FULL MOON IN GEMINI

You will have finally arrived – in terms of achieving the goals you set yourself, in terms of social status, financial security, bonds and relationships. All the activities undertaken between July to September bear fruit, yield dividends now. Ganesha adds a warning: No resting on your laurels, please. Reach out for all that had evaded you, and make definite plans for the future. It's necessary.

30 NOVEMBER: LAST QUARTER IN VIRGO

There is much prestige, power and glory for you, but you're also possessed by a dangerous kind of restlessness. This will need to be kept in check. You will be drawn to occult and arcane practices, a study of tantric precepts, of getting the cosmic energy generated by an awakened kundalini, for example. Know where to draw the line. Have adoration, but also submission to your Lord, your maker.

7 DECEMBER: NEW MOON IN SAGITTARIUS

Perhaps you heeded my advice, as always, inspired by Ganesha. Who else? I submit totally and unconditionally to him. Anyhow, you will be busy building up contacts, not out of necessity or a desire for social climbing but for the sheer joy of it. Librans need human warmth, interaction, relationships. You will be involved with creative pursuits, particularly music and poetry, the arts, and specially the electronic media, like graphic designing, desktop publishing.

15 DECEMBER: FIRST QUARTER IN PISCES

There will be another charge of energy for you, albeit a gentler one. It gives you the sheer energy, vigour and 'go' to once again work hard and spectacularly achieve the most wonderful of results. The results will really be spectacular, but in restrained, quieter, definitely more personal way. By spectacular, I'm using the literal meaning – worth watching!

22 DECEMBER: FULL MOON IN CANCER

The year 2018 draws to a close with a trendsetting quarter, where the millennium is concerned, for Librans. I have pointed out elsewhere, in several articles in fact, but do it again here, that the new millennium actually starts from 2019. Nothing will seem unattainable. You can reach out and touch the stars. Despite these heights seeming to be dizzying, you will have what it takes – the capacity to work at full strength.

29 DECEMBER: LAST QUARTER IN LIBRA

Once again, money, money and more money will be your focus – rentals, taxes, investments, trade and commerce, capital formation. These will all be favoured – also publicity and communications – both the spoken and the written word, ads and campaigns, friends and acquaintances, some romantic interludes, some gains in terms of pleasure.

Achievements 2018

By the grace of Lord Ganesh, my son Nastur found patrons in Shri Raj Kumar Jatia and his son, Shri Adarsh Jatia, the owners of Four Seasons, Mumbai, and Provenance Four Seasons Private Residences. May patience and hard work take my son to the top of the world where Shri Raj Kumar Jatia stands like a shining star. Nastur was graciously invited by the noble business tycoon, Byram Avari, of Avari Group of Hotels, Karachi, and his wife, Goshpi Avari, to attend their fiftieth wedding anniversary.

I bless prosperity upon Prayush Poddar, his father and his family. May his company, AMP Universal Realty Pvt. Ltd, prosper. He has been like a son to me.

May the grace of Lord Ganesha bless Police Commissioner Anupam Singh Gehlot of Rajkot. He has always stood by my family, in good times and bad. Peace and prosperity prevail in Rajkot because of his sincere efforts.

BJP National vice-president and Rajya Sabha member, Vinay Sahasrabuddhe is a very fine and noble gentleman. He was gracious enough to arrange a meeting with Maharashtra chief minister Devendra Fadnavis, who was dynamic and touched by the divine.

Body Language

Ganesha believed astrology to be all about behaviour, relationships and how to handle them. Therefore, the guidelines given below should help you to understand yourself and others. Any information that adds to the knowledge of oneself is always welcome. Here are some examples of body language and its possible interpretations:

POSITIVE VIBES

- Open arms and hands: open and receptive
- Leaning forward: interested in conversation

- Smiling or attempting to be humorous: friendly
- Eye contact with occasional, natural breaks in the stare: focused and curious
- Nodding while listening: attentive and alert
- Open palms: approachable and trusting
- Gesturing with hands while talking: genuinely involved in the conversation
- Upright shoulders: positivity

NEGATIVE VIBES

- Crossed arms and/or legs: closed off, defensive, reserved or suspicious
- Standing with hands inside the pockets: unsure or suspicious
- Fidgeting, running one's tongue along one's teeth, playing with hair

or jewellery or tapping feet: nervous and/or bored

- Lack of eye contact or staring too intently and unblinkingly: untrustworthy
- Leaning back: uncomfortable
- Clasping hands behind the head while leaning back: seeking power
- Drooping shoulders: unsure

Colours of Life

Ganesha believes that life is like a rainbow. Life is like nature, full of abundance and variety. The best part of it is you can actually experiment with the colours given below and have fun. Here, we combine abundance and a variety of colours for joy, use, experience.

- **Energetic:** Red
- **Sporty:** Red, orange
- **Exuberant:** Orange
- **Active:** Orange, yellow
- **Modern:** Yellow

- **Invigorating:** Green, yellow
- **Sunny:** Green, yellow
- **Fresh:** Green
- **Luminous:** Blue, Green
- **Hypnotic:** Blue
- **Regal:** Blue, violet
- **Exotic:** Violet
- **Playful:** Red, orange, violet, yellow
- **Vibrant:** Green, red

(Your astrologer admits that this colour system is *not* his own.)

Important Dates

I have always believed that the fear of failure has never led to advancement of knowledge. These dates and directions may differ from the various trends and forecasts mentioned elsewhere in the book. A different direction is being pursued here. This is a totally different ball game. This is to be taken as an experiment on a mass scale with the readers themselves as guinea pigs (willingly, I hope).

Please remember, as a rule, your birth month and the seventh month from it (including itself) will be hectic. For example, if your birth month is March, the seventh from it will be September. There will be tremendous franticness in both these months.

January: 8–10, 13–15, 18–19, 22–23, 26–27, 31

February: 1, 4–6, 10–11, 14–15, 22–23, 27–28

March: 3–4, 7–9, 12–13, 16–17, 20–21, 30–31

April: 3–5, 8–9, 12–13, 17–18, 20–22, 26–28

May: 5–6, 9–11, 14–15, 19–20, 24–25, 28–30

June: 2–3, 6–7, 10–11,15–16, 20–21, 25–26, 29–30

July: 3–4, 6–7, 10—11, 15–16, 20–21, 25–26, 29–30

August: 1, 4–5, 8–10, 13–15, 18–20, 23–24, 27–28, 31

September: 1, 4–6, 11–13, 15–17, 20–21, 24–25, 27–29

October: 6–8, 12–13, 16–17, 21–22, 24–26, 28–30

November: 2–4, 7–98, 13–14, 17–18, 21–23, 27–29

December: 1–2, 6–7, 10–11, 14–15, 18–20, 23–24, 28–29

Special Note: In January, you will interact with people at home and outside. The period from 21 January to 23 February and from 21 March to 21 April are very special. During 21 May to 20 June expect contacts and travel. Expect friendships and socializing during 21 July to 21 August. From 21 September to 21 October, it will be truly hectic and a time to focus on relationships. From 21 November to 21 December, it is time for trips and ties, the two Ts.

Secret of Life

Ganesha (whom you may refer to as Allah/Christ/Zoroaster or by any other name) is the ignition key of life's car. To start and launch in the name of Ganesha is to assure success and glory. The power, the dazzling light to see visions, have prophetic dreams, and are all bestowed upon us by Ganesha.

Ganesha says the secret of life is in the ability to change with the changing times. In other words, it is the ability to adapt and adjust to situations, conditions, surroundings, climate change, relationships, and science and technology. His second secret is to keep an open mind. Others are most welcome to their own opinion. The third and final secret is to be true to yourself.

Success Secret of No. 17

Ganesha says the secret of life and astrology is to 'Observe! Observe! Observe!' Angela Merkel of Germany, our own Narendra Modi, former US first lady Michelle Obama, and Muhammad Ali, the world's greatest boxer, were all born on the seventeenth days of their birth months. Here is a picture of the tarot card of number seventeen, called the 'Star'. We can see a lady pouring water on the Earth and providing nourishment. To me the lady is the symbol of the great feminine principle which rules the entire world. There are seven stars in the card. As we all know, seven is the mystical number of spirituality, growth and development.

Narendra Modi, 17 September

Michelle Obama, 17 January

Angela Merkel, 17 July

Muhammad Ali, 17 January

To observe is to see completely and carefully. If you observe the above, you will find that all these four individuals are born on the seventeenth. Secondly, the first alphabet of either the first name or the surname in each case is 'M'. The tarot card points towards a great and powerful destiny. Therefore, for all these reasons I believe that the number seventeen and the letter 'M' go with greatness and glory. Yes, I agree that it may not hold true for all the persons born on the seventeenth of various months. I am open-minded.

Is it but a coincidence or is it fate and destiny? I leave it to you to decide.

World Horoscope 2018

Ganesha says cooking is an art. The challenge lies in the ever-changing nature of the ingredients, the temperature, the flavour, the aroma and the very style of cooking.

The ingredients are: artificial intelligence; healing broken bodies, mind, and spirit (most important); managerial skills of a high order; immense strides in medicine and specially brain power; space travel; robots; biopharmaceuticals; origin of life; God vs technology; climate change; and finally the marriage of technology and humanity.

Let me put it in very simple terms. The years from 2018 to 2020 will have both revolution and evolution. Change is the only constant law of nature. Not only will we survive, we will also prevail. The planets responsible for this constant change in direction are Jupiter, Saturn and Pluto. Jupiter means prosperity, Saturn means inevitable changes and Pluto means drastic and unavoidable situations and effects. These three planets are the trio of the cardinal, ambitious, ruthless sign of duty and responsibility: Capricorn. In short, Capricorn is the father who uses a big stick for others but unhappily not for himself. That is the comedy and the tragedy of the Capricorn sign.

As I have said earlier, this is not the right time for Donald Trump. His world view is one that is corrupted by imagination, illusion and, sometimes, hallucination. The Capricorn North Korean President Kim Jong-un will face terrible times and will be completely defeated in the end by fate. Vladimir Putin of Russia and Theresa May of the UK will find it very difficult to hold on to power. Angela Merkel of Germany is simply wonderful and effective. There is a distinct possibility of a settlement or an understanding between the Jews and the Muslims in 2018 itself. God bless them both. Changes in the regimes in Pakistan and the UK appear certain. In the words of Paul Brenton, 'There is peace behind the tumult, goodness behind the evil, happiness behind the agony.' Nobody has a monopoly over truth, love, justice, mercy, kindness and happiness.

India is certainly tolerant up to a certain extent, but it would be wise, practical and necessary to be much more tolerant and far less rigid and orthodox. Water recycling and the treatment of sewage will be a big changer for our country in 2018 and 2019. It will lead to happiness. I say this in all humility and love for Bharat Mata as I am her child. I certainly bow my head at the feet of Bharat Mata. India comes under the planet of Saturn causing changes that are radical, effective, certain. Our Narendra Modi will hold his own against the world. But India will undergo numerous changes, a few of them could be painful but are necessary in the bigger scheme of events. Not religion but responsibility, duty and development will be the three salient features of India in the coming years.

To be happy we must keep an open mind. Perhaps, I say perhaps the best years will be 2018 and 2021. The year 2021 is most certainly the one when science and technology reign supreme and change the very fabric and direction of all of us. Possibly this is the greatest prediction your humble Ganesha devotee will ever make.

Salute and Tribute

A salute and tribute to the following people:

- Gujarat chief minister Vijay Rupani, in whom I saw a perfect balance in the lines of fate, head and heart on his palms. A great heart and a finely tuned mind.
- Philanthropist and naturalist Firdoz Khambhatta, a dangerously handsome, sharp and brilliant man.
- The lovely Meher Medora, firm of purpose and understanding and sympathetic of heart.

- Aravind Mothi and his sister, Anu Mothi, for offering to make a documentary on my life.
- Hotelier Raj Kumar Jatia for his hospitality and courtesy.
- Behram Mehta for his business acumen fused with immense humility and humanity.
- Jay Shah, son of BJP president Amit Shah, for coming to my house and seeking the blessings of all the mighty spirits and energies of each and every religion.
- The very cultured, civilized, and well-informed education minister of Gujarat, Shri Bhupendra Chudasma for his wisdom as well as his faith in Ganesha.
- Usha Nair, Dr Sunny Shah, Nashit Afroze and their team at the International Human Rights Council for services rendered to NGOs all

over the world. I was very humbled to receive a trophy from them, one I shall always treasure.

- Prince Lakshyaraj of Udaipur for his constant endeavour to help thousands of people through education, NGOs and by example for leading an exemplary life.
- My personal blessings by calling upon all the energies of the world to bless my adopted son Chirag and his fiancée Nikita. They are gems.
- I bow very humbly to my guru, Vashishth Mehta, for coaching me across the path of astrology and spirituality.
- Kudos to Neeraj Bajaj, the son of my late friend and patron Ramkrishna Bajaj, and Dadi Mistry for helping the needy, the weak and the helpless in every possible way. Both are truly magnanimous people.

- Raja Vikram Singh of Jambughoda for his humour and resounding laughter. No wonder his Jambughoda resort is doing immensely well.
- Just as this book is going to press, I met Shiroy and his fiancée, Avasti. Avasti specializes in fashion. Shiroy is an absolute gentleman.
- Lastly, I salute and pay my tribute to all those who seek and serve the cause of peace and goodwill to humanity. To me this is certainly the final word.

About the Author

Born on 11 July 1931, Bejan Daruwalla lives with his wife and their three children. Now, eighty-six years old, he is regarded as one of the hundred greatest astrologers of the last century, as acknowledged by *The Millennium Book of Prophecy* (HarperCollins), having accurately predicted the electoral victory of Narendra Modi at the Kanoria Art Centre, Ahmedabad, on 29 March 2012. Bejan featured on *Hard Talk India* on BBC in August 1999. On 10 December 2010, Bejan was featured in *The Job: Corporate Astrologer* in London's *Financial Times*. Bejan was also awarded the Dr Babasaheb Ambedkar Noble Award on 19 April 2017. Giving Bejan more joy and material achievement was shaking hands with His Holiness the Dalai Lama in December 2013, a moment unforgotten and overwhelming. Bejan has one firm belief: tolerance. He believes everyone has the right to their own ideas and opinions; the perspective of others, even and especially if it differs from one's own, must always be respected.

Important Announcement

Our Ganesha devotee Bejan Daruwalla has moved from Mumbai to Ahmedabad. His Ahmedabad address is:

Bejan Daruwalla
Astrologer and Columnist
C/o Nastur Daruwalla
A-5, Spectrum Towers
Opposite Police Stadium
Shahibag
Ahmedabad 380004
India

Telephone
079-32954387
09825470377
08141234275

Email
info@bejandaruwalla.com
bejandaruwalla@rediffmail.com

Website: www.bejandaruwalla.com